So Cute! Baby

Foals

By Julia Jaske

Foals like to play.

Foals like to race.

Foals like to kick.

Foals like to drink.

Foals like to explore.

Foals like to rest.

Foals like to graze.

Foals like to trot.

Foals like to jump.

Foals like to neigh.

Foals like to smile.

Foals like to sleep.

Word List

Foals	explore	neigh
play	rest	smile
race	graze	sleep
kick	trot	
drink	jump	

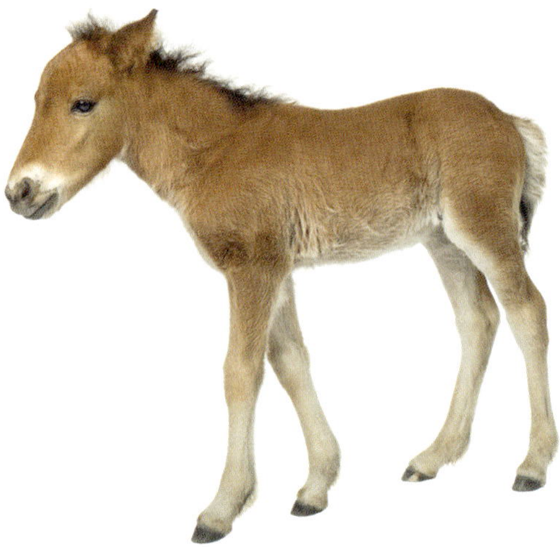

48 Words

Foals like to play.
Foals like to race.
Foals like to kick.
Foals like to drink.
Foals like to explore.
Foals like to rest.
Foals like to graze.
Foals like to trot.
Foals like to jump.
Foals like to neigh.
Foals like to smile.
Foals like to sleep.

CHERRY BLOSSOM PRESS

Published in the United States of America by Cherry Lake Publishing Group
Ann Arbor, Michigan
www.cherrylakepublishing.com

Book Designer: Melinda Millward

Photo Credits: © Brinja Schmidt/Shutterstock, cover, 1; © Katho Menden/Shutterstock, 2; © Olga_i/Shutterstock, 3; © OryPhotography/Shutterstock, 4; © Geza Farkas/Shutterstock, 5; © Iuliia Khabibullina/Shutterstock, 6; © aabeele/Shutterstock, 7; © Alexander D.Sabransky/Shutterstock, 8; © OlesyaNickolaeva/Shutterstock, 9; © Alla-B/Shutterstock, 10; © Liz Miller/Shutterstock, 11; © TamaraLSanchez/Shutterstock, 12; © Plotitsyna NiNa/Shutterstock, 13; © Eric Isselee/Shutterstock, 14

Cherry Blossom Press is an imprint of Cherry Lake Publishing Group.

Library of Congress Cataloging-in-Publication Data

Names: Jaske, Julia, author.
Title: Foals / written by Julia Jaske.
Description: Ann Arbor, Michigan : Cherry Lake Publishing, [2022] | Series: So cute! Baby animals | Title from cover.
Identifiers: LCCN 2022009896 | ISBN 9781668908815 (paperback) | ISBN 9781668913598 (pdf) | ISBN 9781668912003 (ebook)
Subjects: LCSH: Foals—Juvenile literature. | Horses—Juvenile literature
Classification: LCC SF302 .J37 2022 | DDC 636.1—dc23/eng/20220323
LC record available at https://lccn.loc.gov/2022009896

Cherry Lake Publishing Group would like to acknowledge the work of the Partnership for 21st Century Learning, a Network of Battelle for Kids. Please visit http://www.battelleforkids.org/networks/p21 for more information.

Printed in the United States of America
Corporate Graphics